The National Trust's
Cornish Gardens

Photography by Derek Harris

First Published in 2002
by
The WoodLand & Garden Publishing Company,
34 Nene Valley Business Park, Oundle, Peterborough, Cambs, PE8 4HN

Photography Copyright Derek Harris

ISBN 1 899803 16 5

Designed by The WoodLand & Garden Publishing Company

Pictures used in this book, other photographic work and prints by Derek Harris are available from
The WoodLand & Garden Picture Library
34 Nene Valley Business Park, Oundle, Peterborough, Cambs, PE8 4HN.
Tel: 01832 270077   Fax: 01832 270088
Email: derekharris.associates@virgin.net

Cover picture: Spring tulips in the parterre at Lanhydrock

4. Saint Hydroc's Church, Lanhydrock

Introduction

When the National Trust decided to take on the care of gardens, their stated aim was that these gardens should be the very best of their kind.

The National Trust's Cornish gardens are indeed the best of their kind. Cornwall's geography, the Gulf Stream and unique climate, with it's history from the early nineteenth century and the vision of the great Cornish landowners, gardeners and plantsmen have created collections and gardens of great beauty and importance.

Rhododendrons, magnolias, camellias and giant tree ferns brought to Cornwall by Plant Collectors, Patrons and Merchants have created wonderful and exotic gardens unique to Cornwall whilst developing the new cultivars and hybrid's which we enjoy today.

This small souvenir takes a journey from the gardens of Antony and Cotehele in the East via Lanhydrock to Trerice, Trelissick and Glendurgan and on to Trengwainton in the far West.

Derek Harris

Antony House & Garden

and Woodland Garden (Carew Pole Garden Trust)

Torpoint, Cornwall, PL11 2QA

Tel: 01752 812364

5. An eighteenth-century shepherd in an alcove of yew

Antony House

7. View to the river Lynher with spring daffodils

8. Rhododendrons in the Woodland Garden

The Summer Garden

10. The Knot Garden in the enclosed Summer Garden

11. Topiary cone inspiration for the Watercone

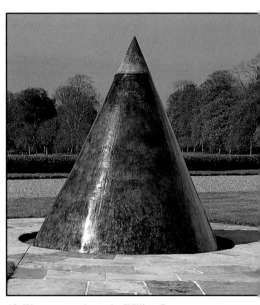

12. Watercone sculpture by William Pye

13. Roses and catmint in the terrace border

14. Detail of terrace border

15. Wild garlic to the Woodland Garden

6. Wild flowers in the Woodland Garden

17. Wild flowers in the Woodland Garden

Cotehele

St Dominick
Saltash
Cornwall PL12 6TA
Tel: 01579 351346

18. East front through rhododendrons

9. East front of the house with formal terrace below

20. View over the combe to Calstock village and the Tamar railway viaduct

21. View into the combe with the dovecote and stewpond

22. Summer house with *Rhododendron* 'Cornish Red'

23. Variegated Japanese Angelica trees on the terrace

24. Daffodil Meadow at Cotehele

25. View of sycamores and daffodils to the house

26. Clematis on wall by east front of house

27. Herbaceous border in the Upper Garden

28. Driftwood Chair

29. Red floribunda roses in the formal terrace

Lanhydrock

Bodmin
Cornwall
PL30 5AD
Tel: 01208 73320

30. Summer view of house and parkland

31. Early morning spring view of the house and parkland

32. *Magnolia campbellii* with mist rolling in from Bodmin

33. Magnolia petals in the Higher Garden

34. Bluebells and azaleas close to the West Path

35. Bluebells and red campion in the wood

37. Red Tulip with forget-me-nots

38. Tulip 'West Point'

39. Tulip 'China Pink'

40. *Camellia japonica*

42. *Camellia japonica* 'Lady Clare'

41. *Camellia x williamsii* 'Glenn's Orbit'

43. *Camellia japonica*

44. Saint Hydroc's church

45. Churchyard border with clematis in late spring

46. Parterre with summer flowering *Begonias*

47. Borlase's stream through the Higher Garden

48. The church of Saint Hydroc

Trerice

Nr Newquay
Cornwall
TR8 4PG
Tel: 01637 875404

49. Urn in rose garden

50. Trerice House

52. The bowling alley border

53. The Rose Garden

54. The Rose Garden

55. Detail in the Rose Garden

Trelissick

Feock
Nr Truro
Cornwall TR3 6QL
Tel: 01872 862090

56. Border of the main lawn

57. Cherry Blossom in Carcaddon

59. Rhododendrons and bluebells near The Dell

60. Path through The Dell

1. *Prunus* 'Kanzan' and 'Taihaku' in Carcaddon

62. Tree Rhododendron on The Woodland Path

63. Colourful border by The Old Kitchen Garden

64. Red Hydrangeas near The Old Kitchen Garden

5. Astilbes in The Dell

66. Colourful border by The Old Kitchen Garden

Glendurgan

Mawnan Smith
Nr Falmouth
Cornwall TR11 5JZ
Tel: 01872 862090

67. Cherry blossom and bluebells

8. View through the valley to the Helford Estuary

70. Maze of Cherry Laurel with the Thatched Summer House

1. Upper Walk with rhododendrons and bluebells

72. The pool with Astilbes and *Cedrus deodara*

73. Valley view with Chusan Palms to the Helford Estuary

74. Rhododendron and Kurume Azalea

75. The Lower Valley

Trengwainton Garden

Penzance
Cornwall
TR20 8RZ
Tel: 01736 362297

76. Primroses by Dawn Redwood

77. Stream Garden along The Drive

78. Tree lined start to The Long Drive

79. Stream Garden with Candelabra Primulas

0. *Acer Palmatum* 'Atropurpureum' with azaleas

81. The Drive

82. *Zantedeschia aethiopica*

83. Rhododendron beneath Tree Fern with bluebells

4. Summer selection along the Stream Garden

85. Colourful border by the Stream Garden

86. Camellia

87. Camellia